# May Sarton
## *A Self-Portrait*

# May Sarton

## *A Self-Portrait*

Edited by

*Marita Simpson and Martha Wheelock*

W · W · NORTON & COMPANY
*New York · London*

The text of this book is composed in Palatino, with display type set in Cloister Openface.

Ishtar Enterprises first published a limited edition of this book in 1982 under the title *World of Light: A Portrait of May Sarton*. This new edition was published in 1986 by W. W. Norton & Company, Inc., New York.

Library of Congress Cataloging-in-Publication Data
Sarton, May, 1912–
May Sarton: a self-portrait.
Rev. ed. of: World of light. 1st ed. c1982.
1. Sarton, May, 1912–       .—Biography. 2. Authors, American—20th century—Biography.
I. Simpson, Marita. II. Wheelock, Martha. III. Sarton, May, 1912—       . World of light. IV. Title.
PS3537.A832Z47 1986   811′1.52 [B]   86–8584

ISBN 0-393-02340-0

W. W. Norton & Company, Inc., 500 Fifth Avenue, New York, N.Y. 10110
W. W. Norton & Company Ltd., 37 Great Russell Street, London WC1B 3NU

1 2 3 4 5 6 7 8 9 0

PUBLISHED

TO

HONOR

*[signature: May Sarton]*

ON THE

OCCASION

OF HER

SEVENTIETH

BIRTHDAY

# CONTENTS

*All the material in this collection has been recorded by May Sarton and is available on a cassette tape through Ishtar*

The material for this book and tape comes from the shooting of the film *World of Light: A Portrait of May Sarton.* For a four-day session in June 1979, May Sarton spontaneously answered our questions about her life and work, and read from her poetry. We fashioned our film from her responses, resulting in the transcript presented here. In addition we have included poems, and some comments not used in the film as a record of Sarton's gifts as a poet and dramatic reader.

With the publication of this cassette tape and book, we celebrate May Sarton's seventieth birthday (May 3, 1982). We thank her for inspiring us to the vision, dedication, and hard work that independent filmmaking demands; we thank her for allowing us this experience to work with her, and above all, for the generous and open gift of herself. In her *Recovering: A Journal* (page 229) Sarton wrote after the film's premiere: "I did have a moment of quiet panic at how much of me has been given away in this film. . . . But I decided that one does not lose one's soul for giving it away."

MARITA SIMPSON
MARTHA WHEELOCK
FILMMAKERS

The Transcript of

# *World Of Light: A Portrait of May Sarton*

*by*
*Marita Simpson   Martha Wheelock*

The form in my life is to keep my center strong and not dispersed. That's what it's all about. It's this very rigid schedule that I follow: three hours in the morning, a walk with the dog, a rest, then a different sort of mental activity or gardening in the afternoon, and early to bed.

I am at my desk from three to four hours every day, and I try to keep that very much, that sacred time, because it's the time when I have energy, it's the morning time. It has to be the morning, before one's mind is all cluttered up, when the door to the subconscious is still open, when you first wake up. That's the creative time for me. Because you want, you see, that *primary intensity*. This is what my life is all about—creating a frame in which I can have that primary intensity for three hours a day. That's all I ask.

It's thought and feeling together, this is what makes the poem for me, when you can think and feel at white heat. And when, of course, the image comes to you which is going to carry this and which is going to help you find out what you're really feeling. This is why I write poems—to find out what I am really feeling.

I never write in form unless I am inspired and when I write in form it is anything but something intellectually worked for. The lines run through my head and I can't stop them. I wrote the whole sequence, the "Divorce of Lovers" sequence, on a lecture trip when I had a high fever a lot of the time and I was terribly exhausted and the poems would just push me. I'd have to get up in the night and write them, write them down, they just flowed through me. This is a case, I think, of real inspiration. It was out of a lot of pain and suddenly the whole thing just came through—in the poems.

I don't write poems very often and they come in batches and it seems to always be connected with a woman in my case who focuses the world for me. Sometimes it's a love affair in the ordinary sense and sometimes it's not. It's simply somebody whom I—well, I say it, I think, quite well—and it's been quoted back to me—in a little passage from *Mrs. Stevens Hears the Mermaids Singing*, when Mar asks the old lady, how can you have loved . . . ? He says, "You can't have loved all those people in the way I mean," the muses, the people she has written for, and she says "I loved them in the way one loves at any age—if it's real at all—obsessively, painfully, with wild exultation; with guilt, with conflict; I wrote poems to and about them; I put them into novels (disguised of course); I brooded upon why they were as they were, so maddening, don't you know? I wrote them ridiculous letters. I lived with their faces. I knew their every gesture by heart. I stalked them like wild animals. I studied them as if they were maps of the world—and in a way I suppose they were . . . . Love opens the doors into everything, as far as I can see, including and perhaps most of all, the door into one's own secret and often terrible and frightening, real self."

It isn't easy to be a woman poet. Partly because one is always seen—and this may be true of the woman writer in general, the woman artist—one is always seen to be a little outside the main stream, not in the center of life. We now can begin to hope that we can be whole human beings, no longer recluses like Emily Dickinson or women with forty lovers, like George Sand.

We have to make myths of our lives or we wouldn't be able to sustain them and I think that this is partly how one handles the monster, really. You are really—you begin, as you get older at least, to know who you are and to choose not to follow paths which go against that image you have of yourself, not the image *projected* necessarily, but the image *you have of yourself*, which says, "success would not be altogether good for me," the image which says, "I live alone and have become a kind of symbol of the woman living alone and it would be a great disappointment to thousands of people if I now got married." Not that I am about to do that. But you do make a myth finally out of your life, especially if you write about it as much as I have.

I often think of that beautiful sentence from Yeats: "Think where man's glory most begins and ends and say my glory was I had such friends." And I feel it very deeply because I was very lucky from the time I was a small child in the people who came into my life in one way or another. Starting with Marie Closset, Jean Dominique, the Belgium poet, who was a teacher in the school where I went for a year and whom I absolutely adored and who recognized in me, I think, a younger version of herself, and we became, of course, very intimate friends, and she's in the first novel. And then, years after that, after my theatre failed and I went to England to start being a writer really and was writing *The Single Hound*, I had the extraordinary luck of meeting the Julian Huxleys, who became very dear friends of mine, both of them and Elizabeth Bowen whom I adored and Virginia Woolf I used to see for tea every time I went over ... Eva LeGallienne, who was a very great influence on me in the theatre and ... well, there are just innumerable people who have been built into my life so that I feel that whatever I am I owe to these people.

I did live, as I said, with one person for a long time. And I loved that communion and that routine and that coming together in the evening and having a drink and talking. This is very precious. I miss it. I am terribly lonely now, but I have also become enamoured of solitude. That's my last great love.

My solitude is everywhere and sometimes I don't speak to anyone, except just to say good morning to the post mistress, for days, for days literally in the winter. And this is hard to handle, to not get unbalanced and not let depression get hold of you. Everything becomes more intense, you see, which is partly why it's marvelous. There's nothing to break the intensity. The great flow from the subconscious to the conscious is the good thing about solitude. There is no barrier between the subconscious and the conscious, or much less than there is if you are talking to a person, when you are constantly taking them into account, especially if you love people as I do.

Life must flow through you at every moment and every day and through every year. You're really a receptacle, an instrument for life to flow through and if you keep stopping it by over control, it's not good. It's not good I mean whether you're a creator or not. So there too I've made a stand on letting feelings out, on honoring one's feelings, even when they may seem to be negative. If you examine anger it has a great deal to teach you and has growth in it, the possibility of growth, if you can face it.

The fact that I've gone on, growing and producing so long and that nothing has stopped me ... the very depressing and discouraging lack of recognition, which really was initially the reason I went to Nelson [N.H.]. And that was nearly twenty years ago. And I went to Nelson saying, "I am a failure really and I am just going to withdraw and work and eventually they'll come to me."

I seemed sentimental—that word has been used—I bitterly resent it because I don't believe that my work is sentimental. As a whole, the vision of life projected in my work is idealistic and humanistic. It is not negative. There's no violence of a person against other people—physical violence—and there's very little sex.... I would like all my work in the end to be transparent and something that is transparent can be very deep, like a well.

It's been a long hard struggle and I think maybe I am a good role model from the point of view of simply persisting and having the psychic energy and the—whatever it is—to go on.

I do get about fifty letters a week. I love hearing from people and the letters have helped me very much because many times when I really felt that the work wasn't getting through—that neither I nor it existed—the fact that people from all over the country, of all ages, men, women and children, wrote me to say, "I've found this book." Years ago it was one book. It was *The Fur Person,* say, then, say, *Kinds of Love* or *As We Are Now* would bring letters from people; in the case of *Kinds of Love,* who loved New England or who had the experience with love in old age, which that is partly about, the failing—the physical failing—and the dealing with it. But now, a very interesting thing has happened. Many of the letters say, "I've read everything you've written and I want to thank you." So it's different from just one book which hits one nerve in a person. And this is, of course, tremendously moving to me and very heartening and helpful, since I still lack serious critical attention.

The journals, funnily enough, have brought me a whole new audience of the young which is extremely charming and amusing to me. I get a great many letters now from young people. Though the journals have seemed to have a rather wide appeal, I don't know why. I've tried to be honest. It's harder than it looks in a book that you know is going to be published to find the right line between indiscretion or between sort of self-exposure in the negative sense *and* to try to give, to be open, to be absolutely open and transparent. Again, the word "transparent" which is very dear to me. I try to be transparent in my human relations and in my work. But, of course, that makes you very vulnerable and few people dare. It's too dangerous.

Poetry and the novel are absolutely different things. You write poetry for yourself, and God, I think and if someone overhears, that's fine. If I were in solitary confinement, I would write poems, but I would not write novels. I think that you write novels as a dialogue really with other people. And also you put characters down into a situation where something is bound to happen which will help you answer a question. Every one of my novels has been written to answer a question, not to tell people something, but to find out what I really think or feel about something.

The journals are a way of finding out where I really am, but in a much more diffused and less intense way. They are not dependent on the muse. They have to do often with encounters with people who come here, who talk to me, or friends whom I see, or the garden. They sort of make me feel that the fabric of my life has a meaning. What often seems fairly meaningless, like weeding a patch in the garden, when I write it into the journal, it sort of becomes something else.

I found it very hard to write about my mother and I was glad when I found an image, a metaphor, which made it possible in this poem called, "An Observation":

True gardeners cannot bear a glove
Between the sure touch and the tender root,
Must let their hands grow knotted as they move
With a rough sensitivity about
Under the earth, between the rock and shoot,
Never to bruise or wound the hidden fruit.
And so I watched my mother's hands grow scarred.
She who could heal the wounded plant or friend
With the same vulnerable yet rigorous love;
I minded once to see her beauty gnarled,
But now her truth is given me to live,
As I learn for myself we must be hard
To move among the tender with an open hand,
And to stay sensitive up to the end
Pay with some toughness for a gentle world.

    I think the deeper you go into the personal, the more universal you are, if you can go deep enough, that's the thing. And if it's no longer just a "look at me, I'm in pain" poem of which I see such an awful lot being written now, that seem to me never to get down to that universal. And, of course, the image is what does it, the image is what does it—the mollusc image, the field, the metaphor is what does it. When you have the metaphor you've got it. "Of Molluscs":

*As the tide rises, the closed mollusc*
*Opens a fraction to the ocean's food,*
*Bathed in its riches. Do not ask*
*What force would do or if force could.*

*A knife is of no use against a fortress.*
*You might break it to pieces as gulls do.*
*No, only the rising tide and its slow progress*
*Opens the shell. Lovers, I tell you true.*

*You who have held yourselves closed hard*
*Against warm sun and wind, shelled up in fears*
*And hostile to a touch or tender word—*
*The ocean rises, salt as unshed tears.*

*Now you are floated on this gentle flood*
*That cannot force or be forced, welcome food*
*Salt as your tears, the rich ocean's blood*
*Eat, rest, be nourished on the tide of love.*

That came after so much pain, and after some very angry poems and then it came, that sense, to wait and let the flood rise.

I think it's a matter of choice that one is a writer, but I think you are chosen to be a poet. You remember, I was in the theatre; I thought I was going to be a theatre person, not a writer, until I was twenty-five really, when my first book of poems came out, but I was always writing poetry even in the theatre years . . . If you are a poet at all, this is a gift like the musical gift or the mathematical gift. You have it very young. Especially if you are lucky enough as I was to have a great teacher when you're young. But as far as being a novelist, that, I think, at least for me, it was a matter of choice. So I think that you are to some extent chosen as a poet and it's a tremendous responsibility.

You have to be willing, as Yeats says, "there's more enterprise in going naked." You finally do have to give something terribly intimate and secret of yourself to the world and not care, because you have to believe that what you have to say is important enough. And I always say to myself, "What difference does it make? In three hundred years I'll either be totally forgotten, which is the more likely or I'll be remembered and if I'll be remembered, what difference does it make, I'll be in the earth, what difference does it make if somebody unearths that I had so many love affairs or that I said this or that to somebody; it doesn't matter because there it is, the living work."

I'm willing to give myself away and take the consequences, whatever they are. And after *Mrs. Stevens* came out, they were considerable. I lost one big job as a result. It was fifteen years ago and people did not come out, you see. I think I have a kind of balance and discretion in the journals and in my work in general that I really don't have unfortunately in my life. But as an artist, I think there's taste in what I'm trying to say. Because that's another thing, a question of taste. What are you going to talk about and what not.

I would like to write now, but I don't know whether I can ... a novel is in some ways like a poem in that you can't decide on purely intellectual grounds, this is a good idea to do this. It's got to come from somewhere very deep and be rather vague, I think. And then it's like seed, and then it grows inside you. It begins to put out leaves and things. I am at a stage now where I have a seed but it hasn't started to grow yet. And the seed would be about women's relationship to women. What's been happening now in the last ten years, which is very moving to me. You see in the women's book stores, you see the way people come and talk to one another and the fact that women have had no place where they could do that. Women of all kinds—nuns come to the women's bookstores, young married women towing little children, women couples come. It's a great place of bonding for women, and something to do with with this, you see it is very vague, is what I want to do next.

So I am just hoping that when it is all added up what will come true is a vision of life and what does one mean when one says that? It is simply that every single human being sees life for himself if he's honest in a way that no one else sees it. And somebody like Virginia Woolf is able to project this extraordinary original vision of life, so that when you open a page of a Virginia Woolf book, you know that that's Virginia Woolf speaking by the way she sees it and I believe this is true to a not-such-a-geniusy extent in my work—that there is a vision of life which is a combination perhaps partly of my European background plus the America I know and plus the temperament, the sort of passionate temperament which is accompanied by a rather critical mind; and this also the critics have not given me credit for, being intelligent as well as sensitive.

It seems to me what's terrifying and marvelous and always

makes for growth is deep feeling and this terrifies Americans. It is one reason why I keep going back to Europe. In Europe the emotional loam is far deeper and people have always taken for granted passionate relationships between women, for instance. My mother was adored by women friends, passionately adored, and it was a generation, probably, that it didn't become sexual. But it is taken for granted that one has these passions and that it was part of growth to have them.

I think that partly the fear of death is because people aren't ready. They haven't had their lives. They suddenly think, but it's limited. What have I done? I've missed everything. I never went to Japan, I never fell in love with anybody, or with anybody outside my marriage, or whatever it may be. I think if you live your life fully, it is exactly like a tree or anything else—you flower, you come into fruit and finally the fruit falls and it's perfectly natural. I feel it in myself. I am definitely much older than I was even a year ago and I rather like it; there's less pressure. I am not quite as driven by the sense that I must produce, produce. I am settling for not writing a book a year, for instance, and then the tempo changes, and this is very satisfactory, if you're ready for it and if you've had enough life so that you don't feel that suddenly it's all gone by and you haven't had any. That's the bad thing, that's the bad thing. Then of course, as I needn't dwell on clichés, the whole ethos in America is the youth ethos, so that the old feel like pariahs. They feel unwanted, and this, I am glad to say, so far has not happened to me, because I still have much to give and people want a lot of me. So I don't feel that when I go out lecturing, you know, to these huge audiences, standing room only nowadays. Oh, it's so moving, you know, I've waited so long for it—when these enormous audiences are there, just like that!!

I don't usually show off these bound books which my kind publishers do for me. I remember when I first met Elizabeth Bowen, I was envious of her row of beautifully bound books in the house in London, and then I had published only one!

This is really just before I left Nelson, when I knew that I was coming here so that there are references to the sea, but also to the hills, where I wrote of course *Plant Dreaming Deep* and *Kinds of Love* and other books to do with New Hampshire.

## Gestalt at Sixty

*For ten years I have been rooted in these hills,*
*The changing light on landlocked lakes,*
*For ten years have called a mountain, friend,*
*Have been nourished by plants, still waters,*
*Trees in their seasons,*
*Have fought in this quiet place*
*For my self.*

I can tell you that first winter
I heard the trees groan.
I heard the fierce lament
As if they were on the rack under the wind.
I too have groaned here,
Wept the wild winter tears.
I can tell you that solitude
Is not all exaltation, inner space
Where the soul breathes and work can be done.
Solitude exposes the nerve,
Raises up ghosts.
The past, never at rest, flows through it.

Who wakes in a house alone
Wakes to moments of panic.
(Will the roof fall in?
Shall I die today?)
Who wakes in a house alone
Wakes to inertia sometimes,
To fits of weeping for no reason.
Solitude swells the inner space
Like a balloon.
We are wafted hither and thither
On the air currents.
How to land it?

I worked out anguish in a garden.
Without the flowers,
The shadow of trees on snow, their punctuation,
I might not have survived.
I came here to create a world
As strong, renewable, fertile,
As the world of nature all around me—
Learned to clear myself as I have cleared the pasture,
Learned to wait,
Learned that change is always in the making
(Inner and outer) if one can be patient,
Learned to trust myself.

*The house is receptacle of a hundred currents.*
*Letters pour in,*
*Rumor of the human ocean, never at rest,*
*Never still…*
*Sometimes it deafens and numbs me.*

*I did not come here for society*
*In these years*
*When every meeting is collision,*
*The impact huge,*
*The reverberations slow to die down.*
*Yet what I have done here*
*I have not done alone,*
*Inhabited by a rich past of lives,*
*Inhabited also by the great dead,*
*By music, poetry—*
*Yeats, Valery stalk through this house.*
*No day passes without a visitation—*
*Rilke, Mozart.*
*I am always a lover here,*
*Seized and shaken by love.*

*Lovers and friends,*
*I come to you starved*
*For all you have to give,*
*Nourished by the food of solitude,*
*A good instrument for all you have to tell me,*
*For all I have to tell you.*
*We talk of first and last things,*
*Listen to music together,*
*Climb the long hill to the cemetery*
*In autumn,*
*Take another road in spring*
*Toward newborn lambs.*

*No one comes to this house*
*Who is not changed.*
*I meet no one here who does not change me.*

How rich and long the hours become,
How brief the years,
In this house of gathering,
This life about to enter its seventh decade.

I live like a baby
Who bursts into laughter
At a sunbeam on the wall,
Or like a very old woman
Entranced by the prick of stars
Through the leaves.

And now, as the fruit gathers
All the riches of summer
Into its compact world,
I feel richer than ever before,
And breathe a larger air.

I am not ready to die,
But I am learning to trust death
As I have trusted life.
I am moving
Toward a new freedom
Born of detachment,
And a sweeter grace—
Learning to let go.

I am not ready to die,
But as I approach sixty
I turn my face toward the sea.
I shall go where tides replace time,
Where my world will open to a far horizon
Over the floating, never-still flux and change.
I shall go with the changes,
I shall look far out over golden-grasses
And blue waters . . . .

There are no farewells.

Wheelock:
What do you want to be remembered for, as a writer and as a person?

Sarton:
Oh Goodness, I don't know. I guess for being fully human, if I am.

# MAY
# OFF CAMERA

# On the Poet & Poetry

# My Sisters, O My Sisters

*Nous qui voulions poser, image ineffaceable*
*Comme un delta divin notre main sur le sable*

Anna de Noailles

## 1

*Dorothy Wordsworth, dying, did not want to read,*
*"I am too busy with my own feelings," she said.*

*And all women who have wanted to break out*
*Of the prison of consciousness to sing or shout*

*Are strange monsters who renounce the treasure*
*Of their silence for a curious devouring pleasure.*

*Dickinson, Rossetti, Sappho—they all know it,*
*Something is lost, strained, unforgiven in the poet.*

*She abdicates from life or like George Sand*
*Suffers from the mortality in an immortal hand,*

*Loves too much, spends a whole life to discover*
*She was born a good grandmother, not a good lover.*

*Too powerful for men: Madame de Stael. Too sensitive:*
*Madame de Sévigné, who burdened where she meant to give.*

Delicate as that burden was and so supremely lovely,
It was too heavy for her daughter, much too heavy.

Only when she built inward in a fearful isolation
Did any one succeed or learn to fuse emotion

With thought. Only when she renounced did Emily
Begin in the fierce lonely light to learn to be.

Only in the extremity of spirit and the flesh
And in renouncing passion did Sappho come to bless.

Only in the farewells or in old age does sanity
Shine through the crimson stains of their mortality.

And now we who are writing women and strange monsters
Still search our hearts to find the difficult answers,

Still hope that we may learn to lay our hands
More gently and more subtly on the burning sands.

To be through what we make more simply human,
To come to the deep place where poet becomes woman,

Where nothing has to be renounced or given over
In the pure light that shines out from the lover,

In the warm light that brings forth fruit and flower
And that great sanity, that sun, the feminine power.

Sarton:

I am trying to find out through the means of a strong metaphor what has really happened. It's the metaphor that teaches you. It's the metaphor that comes from the subconscious; and then the music. When they come together I know I'm inspired. For me the Muse has been always a woman. Although I have loved men, I haven't written poems to them. It's very mysterious. It is not something you can control. It does come from the subconscious, from the Gods, if you will. It occurs to me that the poem to read at this moment, because of the finding of one's own secret and terrible self through encounter is "The Muse as Medusa." In this case the Muse was a woman whom I hardly every saw, so it was not a love affair:

# The Muse as Medusa

I saw you once, Medusa; we were alone.
I looked you straight in the cold eye, cold.
I was not punished, was not turned to stone—
How to believe the legends I am told?

I came as naked as any little fish.
Prepared to be hooked, gutted, caught;
But I saw you, Medusa, made my wish,
And when I left you I was clothed in thought . . .

Being allowed, perhaps, to swim my way
Through the great deep and on the rising tide,
Flashing wild streams, as free and rich as they,
Though you had power marshaled on your side.

The fish escaped to many a magic reef;
The fish explored many a dangerous sea—
The fish, Medusa, did not come to grief,
But swims still in a fluid mystery.

Forget the image: your silence is my ocean,
And even now it teems with life. You choose
To abdicate by total lack of motion,
But did it work, for nothing really froze?

Is it all fluid still, that world of feeling
Where thoughts, those fishes, silent, feed and rove;
And, fluid, it is also full of healing,
For love is healing, even rootless love.

I turn your face around! It is my face.
That frozen rage is what I must explore—
Oh secret, self-enclosed, and ravaged place!
This is the gift I thank Medusa for.

43

I start a poem by making notes in long hand on a pad. What the notes give me is the image, which comes, as I said, from the subconscious, is not deliberate, and is usually accompanied by the sound, the rhythm—whether it's going to be in meter or free verse; then I start working with that. Of course, you have to be in a state of "White Heat," intellectually and emotionally at the same time. I think the poem that suggests what I'm talking about is "Prisoner at a Desk."

# Prisoner at a Desk

It is not so much trying to keep alive
As trying to keep from blowing apart
From inner explosions every day.
I sit here, open to psychic changes,
Living myself as if I were a land,
Or mountain weather, the quick cycles
Where we are tossed from the ice age
To bursts of spring, to sudden torrents
Of rain like tears breaking through iron.
It is all I can do to keep tethered down.

No prisoner at a desk, but an ocean
Or forest where waves and gentle leaves
And strange wild beasts under the groves
And whales in all their beauty under the blue
Can gently rove together, still untamed,
Where all opens and breathes and can grow.

Whatever I have learned of good behavior
Withers before these primal powers.
Here at the center governess or censor
No longer has command. The soul is here,
Inviolable splendor that exists alone.

Prisoner at a desk? No, universe of feeling
Where everything is seen, and nothing mine
To plead with or possess, only partake of,
As if at times I could put out a hand
And touch the lion head, the unicorn.
Here there is nothing, no one, not a sound
Except the distant rumor, the huge cloud
Of archetypal images that feed me . . .

Look, there are finches at the feeder.
My parrot screams with fear at a cloud.
Hyacinths are budding. Light is longer.

I think that whatever moves one should go into the work. But if a poem is simply rhetoric, there's a danger. Then people think you're screaming at them. Why don't I read "At Kent State?" That, of course, came out of deep feeling. It is an example, by the way, of how one can use form. I have used as the rhythm a nursery rhyme, "We'll to the woods no more, the laurels are cut down" ("Nous n'irons plus aux bois; les lauriers sont coupés."), which every French schoolchild knows by heart. Partly it made me keep a very short line; it made me keep the tension:

## "We'll to the Woods No More, the Laurels Are Cut Down"

## AT KENT STATE

*The war games are over,*
*The laurels are cut down.*
*We'll to the woods no more*
*With live ammunition*
*To murder our own children*
*Because they hated war.*

*The war games are over.*
*How many times the pain*
*We were given a choice—*
*"Sick of the violence"*
*(Oh passionate human voice!)—*
*But buried it again.*

*The war games are over.*
*Virile, each stood alone—*
*John, Robert, Martin Luther.*
*Still we invoke the gun,*
*Still make a choice for murder,*
*Bury the dead again.*

*The war games are over,*
*And all the laurel's gone.*
*Dead warrior, dead lover,*
*Was the war lost or won?*
*What say you, blasted head?*
No answer from the dead.

We talked about the whole work and the poet as separate in some way from the novelist. The poem I would like to read now, which is called "Proteus," is about what it is like to be a poet. I am criticized for keeping the Hell out, yet I feel that perhaps one wants to transcend the Hell and this is part of what poetry is about:

# Proteus

*They were intense people, given to migraine,*
*Outbursts of arrogance, self-pity, or wild joy,*
*Affected by the weather like a weather vane,*
*Hungry for glory, exhausted by each day,*
*Humble at night and filled with self-distrust.*
*Time burned their heels. They ran because they must—*

*Sparkled, spilled over in the stress of living.*
*Oh, they were fickle, fluid, sometimes cruel,*
*Who still imagined they were always giving;*
*And the mind burned experience like fuel,*
*So they were sovereign losers, clumsy winners,*
*And read the saints, and knew themselves as sinners.*

*Wild blood subdued, it was pure form they blest.*
*Their sunlit landscapes were painted across pain.*
*They dreamed of peaceful gardens and of rest—*
*And now their joys, their joys alone remain.*
*Transparent, smiling, like calm gods to us,*
*Their names are Mozart, Rilke—Proteus.*

You are finding something out by writing the poem, and when you finish it, you have a tremendous sense of relief and of having grown. And more than that, I often feel that my poems are a little ahead of where I am; they tell me. "My poems tell me where I have to go"—is a line I have often said to myself but never made into a poem.

On
Love

"A Light Left On." I love to read this. It was written for Judith Matlack with whom I lived for many years and for whom I did not write a great many poems, I am sorry to say. But I did write this one.

# A Light Left On

In the evening we came back
Into our yellow room,
For a moment taken aback
To find the light left on,
Falling on silent flowers,
Table, book, empty chair
While we had gone elsewhere,
Had been away for hours.

When we came home together
We found the inside weather.
All of our love unended
The quiet light demanded,
And we gave, in a look
At yellow walls and open book,
The deepest world we share
And do not talk about
But have to have, was there,
And by that light found out.

This next one is a more complex poem. It was written for Elizabeth Bowen, with whom I was briefly in love, and whom I admired and adored and saw a great deal in the 1930's. The image at the end comes from Henry James, who uses it, I think, about the novel, that it has to be like a glass of water which is absolutely full, but does not spill over. I love that image:

# Because What I Want Most Is Permanence

Because what I want most is permanence,
The long unwinding and continuous flow
Of subterranean rivers out of sense,
That nourish arid landscapes with their blue—
Poetry, prayer, or call it what you choose
That frees the complicated act of will
And makes the whole world both intense and still—
I set my mind to artful work and craft,
I set my heart on friendship, hard and fast
Against the wild inflaming wink of chance
And all sensations opened in a glance.
Oh blue Atlantis where the sailors dream
Their girls under the waves and in the foam—
I move another course. I'll not look down.

Because what I most want is permanence,
What I do best is bury fire now,
To bank the blaze within, and out of sense,
Where hidden fires and rivers burn and flow,
Create a world that is still and intense.
I come to you with only the straight gaze.
These are not hours of fire but years of praise,
The glass full to the brim, completely full,
But held in balance so no drop can spill.

I would now like to read a poem called "In Time Like Air." Sometimes you get a metaphor that is so powerful that you can't even use it at the time but you know that it is going to come in and be exactly what you need in years later. This image comes from Gaston Bachelard, the French psychoanalyst of the Image who has written a series of books which are fascinating. The first was *La Psychanalyse Du Feu, The Psychoanalysis of Fire;* then *L'Eau et les Rêves, Water and Dreams;* I've forgotten the title of the one about Earth, which this wonderful image of salt comes from. He says that salt is a Janus material; it crystallizes in air and dissolves in water. I made a note of this in a notebook. I then encountered somebody whom I was very moved by, but it never became a love affair. This poem was written at the beginning of being fascinated by a person. I found that the image was just right. This is a metaphysical poem, and I'm rather fond of it. It has quite a tight form:

# In Time Like Air

*Consider the mysterious salt:*
*In water it must disappear.*
*It has no self. It knows no fault.*
*Not even sight may apprehend it.*
*No one may gather it or spend it.*
*It is dissolved and everywhere.*

*But out of water into air,*
*It must resolve into a presence,*
*Precise and tangible and here.*
*Faultlessly pure, faultlessly white,*
*It crystallizes in our sight*
*And has defined itself to essence.*

*What element dissolves the soul*
*So it may be both found and lost,*
*In what suspended as a whole?*
*What is the element so blest*
*That there identity can rest*
*As salt in the clear water cast?*

*Love, in its early transformation,*
*And only love, may so design it*
*That the self flows in pure sensation,*
*Is all dissolved, and found at last*
*Without a future or a past,*
*And a whole life suspended in it.*

*The faultless crystal of detachment*
*Comes after, cannot be created*
*Without the first intense attachment,*
*Even the saints achieve this slowly;*
*For us, more human and less holy,*
*In time like air is essence stated.*

You always think that once you've arrived at some place, that you're going to be there forever. I wrote this poem, "Myself to Me," when I thought I was too old for love. That was some years ago. I've learned better now:

# Myself to Me

*"Set the table and sweep the floor—*
*Love will not come back to this door.*

*Plant your bulbs, now summer flowers.*
*These be your joys, these your powers.*

*A cat for comfort, wood to burn,*
*And changing light as seasons turn.*

*Long hours alone and work to do—*
*These are your strength. These are for you."*

*So spoke myself, I listened well;*
*I thought that self had truth to tell.*

*But love came back after many a year,*
*Love all unasked knocked at the door.*

*Love all unasked broke down the door.*
*To bring me pain as it did before,*

*To bring me back lost poetry,*
*And all I'd meant alone to be.*

*What does myself now say to me?*
*"Open the door to Mystery.*

*Gather the grapes from any vine,*
*And make rich wine, and make rich wine.*

*Out of the passion comes the form,*
*And only passion keeps it warm.*

*Set the table, sweep the floor—*
*Forget the lies you told before."*

These two poems, written roughly at the same time, are a part of a sonnet sequence "The Autumn Sonnets." I was learning a lot about love in this period:

## #2

If I can let you go as trees let go
Their leaves, so casually, one by one;
If I can come to know what they do know,
That fall is the release, the consummation,
Then fear of time and the uncertain fruit
Would not distemper the great lucid skies
This strangest autumn, mellow and acute.
If I can take the dark with open eyes
And call it seasonal, not harsh or strange
(For love itself may need a time of sleep),
And, treelike, stand unmoved before the change,
Lose what I lose to keep what I can keep,
The strange root still alive under the snow,
Love will endure—if I can let you go.

## #11

For steadfast flame wood must be seasoned,
And if love can be trusted to last out,
Then it must first be disciplined and reasoned
To take all weathers, absences, and doubt.
No resinous pine for this, but the hard oak
Slow to catch fire, would see us through a year.
We learned to temper words before we spoke,
To force the furies back, learned to forbear,
In silence to wait out erratic storm,
And bury tumult when we were apart.
The fires were banked to keep a winter warm
With heart of oak instead of resinous heart,
And in this testing year beyond desire
Began to move toward durable fire.

On
Nature

"June Wind." This was an extraordinary day when the grass was much longer than it is now and the wind made waves in the field whereas the ocean beyond it was absolutely flat, as it rarely is:

## June Wind

*I watched wind ripple the field's supple grasses.*
*For once earth is alive while restless ocean*
*Lies still beyond it like a flat blue screen.*
*I watch the wind burnishing as it passes,*
*Lifting soft waves, an ecstasy of motion,*
*A long glissando through the static green.*

*These waves crash on no rock; rooted, they stay,*
*As restless love, that ocean, changes over*
*And comes to land, alive, a shining field*
*Caught in wind's captivating gentle play*
*As though a harp played by a subtle lover—*
*And the tormented ocean has been stilled.*

# After the Storm

*The roar of big surf and above it all night*
*The peepers singing out so sweet and frail!*
*Above the pounding roar that wears down rock*
*They dare, they try to connect through the gale.*
*And if that relentless boom might seem to mock*
*Those who still risk their hope before daylight,*
*That song suggests something is going right.*
*Whatever locked love cannot bear to do,*
*The tree frogs can, and spring is breaking through.*

# Easter Morning

## (read at a rehearsal in the Library of Congress)

*The extreme delicacy of this Easter morning*
*Spoke to me as a prayer and as a warning.*
*It was light on the brink, spring light*
*After a train that gentled my dark night.*
*I walked through landscapes I had never seen*
*Where the fresh grass had just begun to green,*
*And its roots, watered deep, sprung to my tread;*
*The maples wore a cloud of feathery red,*
*But flowering trees still showed their clear design*
*Against the pale blue brightness chilled like wine.*
*And I was praying all the time I walked,*
*While starlings flew about, and talked, and talked.*
*Somewhere and everywhere life spoke the word.*
*The dead trees woke; each bush held its bird.*
*I prayed for delicate love and difficult,*
*That all be gentle now and know no fault,*
*That all be patient—as a wild rabbit fled*
*Sudden before me. Dear love, I would have said*
*(And to each bird who flew up from the wood),*
*I would be gentler still if that I could,*
*For on this Easter morning it would seem*
*The softest footfall danger is, extreme...*
*And so I prayed to be less than the grass*
*And yet to feel the Presence that might pass.*
*I made a prayer, I heard the answer, "Wait,*
*When all is so in peril, and so delicate!"*

Talking about sound, the particular sound of poetry, I'd like to read a poem which might be called a pure lyric. These are poems which come rarely, I think, to any poet, and which are always very precious. They somehow seem like gifts. So here it is. This is a picnic in Italy, under olive trees, that wonderful silvery light, silvery leaves. It is called "The Olive Grove:"

## The Olive Grove

*Here in the olive grove,*
*Under the cobalt dome,*
*The ancient spirits move*
*And light comes home,*

*And nests in silvery leaves.*
*It makes each branch a cloud,*
*And comes and goes, and weaves*
*Aerial song aloud.*

*Here every branch is gifted*
*With spiritual fruit*
*And every leaf is lifted*
*To brightness from the root.*

*Where the terrestrial plane*
*Meets vision and desire,*
*The silver and the green*
*Are strung on a great lyre,*

*And leafy seraphim*
*The sun and shade among*
*Turn each grove to a hymn;*
*Whole hillsides are in song.*

*Silvery, shadowy now*
*The fruit over our head,*
*Who lie and hardly know*
*Which is light, which is bread*

# On Sarton's Parents

As I said, I found it very hard to write poems about my mother. This poem is about her death. I wrote it immediately afterwards, but didn't publish it for some years. She died of cancer. It is really a poem about letting go too, in a way:

## A Hard Death

*We have seen how dignity can be torn*
*From the naked dying or the newly born*
*By a loud voice or an ungentle presence,*
*Harshness of haste or lack of reverence;*
*How the hospital nurse may casually unbind*
*The suffering body from the lucid mind.*
*The spirit enclosed in that fragile shell*
*Cannot defend itself, must endure all.*
*And not only the dying, helpless in a bed,*
*Ask for a little pillow for the head,*
*A sip of water, a cool hand to bless:*
*The living have their lonely agonies.*
*"Is there compassion?" a friend asked me.*
*"Does it exist in another country?"*

*The busy living have no time to see*
*The flowers, so silent and so alive,*
*That paling to lavender of the anemone,*
*That purpling of the rose no one can save,*
*Dying, but at each second so complete*
*A photograph would show no slightest change,*
*Only the human eye, imperfect but aware,*
*Knows that the flower arrested on the air*
*Is flying through space, doing a dance*
*Toward the swift fall of petals, all at once.*

God's Grace, given freely, we do not deserve,
But we can choose at least to see its ghost
On every face. Oh, we can wish to serve
Each other gently as we live, though lost.
We cannot save, be saved, but we can stand
Before each presence with gentle heart and hand;
Here in this place, in this time without belief,
Keep the channels open to each other's grief;
Never accept a death or life as strange
To its essence, but at each second be aware
How God is moving always through each flower
From birth to death in a multiple gesture
Of abnegation, and when the petals fall
Say it is beautiful and good, say it is well.

I saw my mother die and now I know
The spirit cannot be defended. It must go
Naked even of love at the very end.
"Take the flowers away" (Oh, she had been their friend!),
And we who ached could do nothing more—
She was detached and distant as a star.

Let us be gentle to each other this brief time
For we shall die in exile far from home,
Where even the flowers can no longer save
Only the living can be healed by love.

"My Father's Death." He died about seven years after my mother; he died in the very fullness of his power. It was a wonderful death, and I felt set free by it. I think you only become yourself when both your parents are dead. It's a terrible thing to say, but it's true. And that's what this poem is about:

# My Father's Death

*After the laboring birth, the clean stripped hull*
*Glides down the ways and is gently set free,*
*The landlocked, launched; the cramped made bountiful—*
*Oh, grave great moment when ships take the sea!*
*Alone now in my life, no longer child,*
*This hour and its flood of mystery,*
*Where death and love are wholly reconciled,*
*Launches the ship of all my history.*
*Accomplished now is the last struggling birth,*
*I have slipped out from the embracing shore*
*Nor look for comfort to maternal earth.*
*I shall not be a daughter any more,*
*But through this final parting, all stripped down,*
*Launched on the tide of love, go out full grown.*

On
Inner Space

I have a great feeling, of course, about the Dutch painters because of my having been born in Belgium; it's in my blood. The apparent calm of these paintings holds in it so much feeling. Just look at the hands in a Memling virgin—marvelously sensitive hands. This poem was inspired by Pieter de Hooch. He is not as great a painter as Vermeer, but he has such strong feeling about the domestic scene. I've looked at many of his paintings, hard, and felt affinities:

# Dutch Interior

## Pieter de Hooch (1629-1682)

*I recognize the quiet and the charm,*
*This safe enclosed room where a woman sews*
*And life is tempered, orderly, and calm.*

*Through the Dutch door, half-open, sunlight streams*
*And throws a pale square down on the red tiles.*
*The cosy black dog suns himself and dreams.*

*Even the bed is sheltered, it encloses,*
*A cupboard to keep people safe from harm,*
*Where copper glows with the warm flush of roses.*

*The atmosphere is all domestic, human,*
*Chaos subdued by the sheer power of need.*
*This is a room where I have lived as woman,*

*Lived too what the Dutch painter does not tell—*
*The wild skies overhead, dissolving, breaking,*
*And how that broken light is never still,*

*And how the roar of waves is always near,*
*What bitter tumult, treacherous and cold,*
*Attacks the solemn charm year after year!*

*It must be felt as peace won and maintained*
*Against those terrible antagonists—*
*How many from this quiet room have drowned?*

*How many left to go, drunk on the wind,*
*And take their ships into heartbreaking seas;*
*How many whom no woman's peace could bind?*

*Bent to her sewing, she looks drenched in calm.*
*Raw grief is disciplined to the fine thread.*
*But in her heart this woman is the storm;*

*Alive, deep in herself, holds wind and rain,*
*Remaking chaos into an intimate order*
*Where sometimes light flows through a window pane.*

# About May Sarton

By her seventieth birthday, the occasion for the publication of the limited edition of this book, titled *World of Light: A Portrait of May Sarton*, she had written eleven volumes of poetry, sixteen novels (plus a new one due out in Fall 1982), and six books of memoirs and journals. By now, 1986, she has published three more volumes of poetry, two more novels, and three more books of memoirs and journals.

On May 3, 1912, May Sarton was born in Belgium to two extraordinary parents. Her father, George Sarton, was an historian of science, an author and a Harvard professor; her mother, Mabel, an artist and designer. The family moved to America when May was two years old and settled in Cambridge, Massachusetts. After high school May Sarton joined Eva Le Gallienne's Civic Repertory Theatre Company. Two years later she formed her own theatre company and worked with them as director, actress and producer for four more years. During this time, May was also writing poetry, and once her first book of poems, *Encounter in April*, was published in 1937, Sarton was totally committed to writing. She now resides and writes on the coast of Maine, where the film *World of Light: A Portrait of May Sarton* was filmed.

Thanks are due to May Sarton, poet and copyright owner, for permission to print certain of her poems in this volume:

"An Observation," "My Sisters, O My Sisters," "A Light Left On," "Because What I Want Most Is Permanence," "The Olive Grove," "In Time Like Air," "My Father's Death," "'We'll to the Woods No More, the Laurels Are Cut Down'," "Gestalt at Sixty," "Myself to Me," "The Autumn Sonnets," "Prisoner at a Desk," "The Muse as Medusa," "Proteus," "Easter Morning," "A Hard Death," "Dutch Interior," from *Collected Poems*, by May Sarton, copyright 1974, W. W. Norton & Company, Inc., 500 Fifth Avenue, New York, N.Y. 10110.

"O Molluscs," "June Wind," "After the Storm," from *Halfway to Silence*, by May Sarton, copyright 1980, W. W. Norton & Company, Inc., 500 Fifth Avenue, New York, N.Y. 10110.

# Photographic Credits

<table>
<tr><td>Lotte Jacobi</td><td>back flap.</td></tr>
<tr><td>Barbara Murphy</td><td>page 18.</td></tr>
<tr><td>Jill Krementz</td><td>page 36.</td></tr>
</table>

Information on the film,
*World of Light: A Portrait of May Sarton,*
may be obtained from:

Ishtar Films
Box 51
Patterson, New York 12563
(914) 878-3561

It is available on 16 mm for sale or rental; and on ¾"
and ½" (VHS or Beta) VIDEO for sale.